Tiberius

A Captivating Guide to the Life of Ancient Rome's Second Emperor and How He Ruled the Roman Empire

© **Copyright 2019**

All Rights Reserved. No part of this book may be reproduced in any form without permission in writing from the author. Reviewers may quote brief passages in reviews.

Disclaimer: No part of this publication may be reproduced or transmitted in any form or by any means, mechanical or electronic, including photocopying or recording, or by any information storage and retrieval system, or transmitted by email without permission in writing from the publisher.

While all attempts have been made to verify the information provided in this publication, neither the author nor the publisher assumes any responsibility for errors, omissions or contrary interpretations of the subject matter herein.

This book is for entertainment purposes only. The views expressed are those of the author alone, and should not be taken as expert instruction or commands. The reader is responsible for his or her own actions.

Adherence to all applicable laws and regulations, including international, federal, state and local laws governing professional licensing, business practices, advertising and all other aspects of doing business in the US, Canada, UK or any other jurisdiction is the sole responsibility of the purchaser or reader.

Neither the author nor the publisher assumes any responsibility or liability whatsoever on the behalf of the purchaser or reader of these materials. Any perceived slight of any individual or organization is purely unintentional.

Free Bonus from Captivating History (Available for a Limited time)

Hi History Lovers!

Now you have a chance to join our exclusive history list so you can get your first history ebook for free as well as discounts and a potential to get more history books for free! Simply visit the link below to join.

Captivatinghistory.com/ebook

Also, make sure to follow us on Facebook, Twitter and Youtube by searching for Captivating History.

Contents

INTRODUCTION 1

CHAPTER 1 – BEFORE THE EMPERORS 3

CHAPTER 2 – BORN INTO TURMOIL 8

CHAPTER 3 – THE EYE OF THE EMPEROR 13

CHAPTER 4 – IN THE SHADOW OF AUGUSTUS 17

CHAPTER 5 – FIRST CONQUEST 23

CHAPTER 6 – FORCED MARRIAGE 26

CHAPTER 7 – ROCK BOTTOM 30

CHAPTER 8 – ASCENSION 35

CHAPTER 9 – A SLIPPERY SLOPE TO CAPRI 38

CHAPTER 10 – THE LAST JAVELIN 42

CONCLUSION 45

SOURCES 49

Introduction

Tiberius Claudius Nero Caesar.

Compared with the preceding rulers, Julius Caesar and Augustus, the name does not ring out with the same fame and pomposity. Shakespeare wrote no plays about Tiberius; his name does not echo in the history books with the same awe-inspiring prominence. Even his successors, Caligula and Nero, are more famous than he was. In fact, Tiberius can hardly be called famous at all. History knows him more for his infamy.

Tiberius is remembered, if he is remembered at all, for his bad behavior. He spent much of his rule on a Greek island surrounded by every pleasure that his diseased flesh could dream of, abandoning his empire to scandal and intrigue. He is a great villain of Roman history.

That same history has taught us, however, that even the worst of its villains are not born. They are made, forged in the brutal fire of suffering and beaten into the shape of despots and tyrants by the unrelenting hammer of cruelty. The same hardship that creates history's heroes also has a tendency to shape its villains, and Tiberius is no exception.

The story of the life of Rome's second emperor should, at first glance, evoke disgust and horror. Instead, as one pages through one sorry chapter after another, an unexpected emotion makes itself known: pity. The life of this man is a sorry soap opera of family drama, with the victim time and time again turning out to be Tiberius. His parents were forced to divorce when he was a little boy. His own marriage would, in fact, suffer the same fate, and he would end up married to a woman that the whole empire hated. His own brother died in his arms. His son was taken from him. Even his last and best friend died young, and Tiberius was wrongfully accused of killing him.

This is not just the story of a despotic ruler who abandoned his post when the empire needed him and decided to, instead, descend into unspeakable sexual horrors. This is the story of a man who was beaten, broken by life. A man who felt he had no other choice.

Chapter 1 – Before the Emperors

According to legend, the first king of Rome was raised by a she-wolf.

As helpless babies, Romulus and his twin brother Remus were cast out into the wilderness by a jealous and vengeful king. Set adrift in a basket on the banks of the Tiber, the two babies were doomed to die. But legend has it that they were both the sons of Mars, the Roman god of war, and they would not be so easily dispatched. A she-wolf rescued the two babies and raised them like they were her own cubs until they were able to care for themselves. The two brothers became warriors, seeking vengeance on the king that had tried to kill them. They took their revenge and then, in defiance, founded a city on the banks of the very river that was supposed to have drowned them.

But this city was not big enough for both of them. Conflict arose between the brothers, and they came to blows. Remus was killed, and when Romulus emerged as the victor, he knew what to name the city. He named it after himself: Rome.

The legend tells that Romulus became the first king of Rome in the mid-8th century BCE. It's more likely that Rome had existed for years as a meaningless little village, and that an invasion from the neighboring Etruscans had forced its people and the tribes surrounding it to stand together and defend their homes. Either way, we have records of the first seven kings of Rome, who lived between 735 and 510 BCE.

These kings were very different from those ruling the tribes and countries that surrounded them for one main reason: the kingdom of Rome was not a hereditary one. Even though Rome's ruler was called *rex*, or "king," he did not ascend to his throne by birthright. Instead, he was nominated by a chosen and trusted citizen of Rome and then elected by a council known as the Curiate Assembly.

Although the king was elected, he still ruled as an absolute monarch. He was the religious, military, and administrative leader of Rome, and the people had no say in their fates.

The kingdom of Rome prospered under the first few kings. Romulus' successor, Numa Pompilius, was a gentle and pious man, which was a sharp contrast to the brutal founder of Rome. The kings to follow were warriors, however, and they fought to expand and unify Rome. What had once been a village grew up into an important city with a large population and a powerful government. However, the king's word was still law—and when the kings were unjust, the people suffered.

The last king of Rome was the most unjust of them all. Lucius Tarquinius Superbus, or Tarquin the Proud, assassinated his predecessor, seized power, and—according to legend—became a despicable tyrant. The people suffered under his harsh rule but not for long. When Tarquinius' son, Sextus, attacked and raped a beloved and virtuous woman named Lucretia (who committed suicide as a result), the people viewed this as an unforgivable sin. Tarquinius was forced out by his own government and sent into exile. Despite allying with the Etruscans in a bid to take Rome back, Tarquinius would never sit on its throne again.

Tarquinius' tyrannical rule had left the Roman people wary of ever trusting a king again. In fact, monarchy was out of the question for the majority of the people, who had realized that they had the power to overthrow their leaders if they so pleased. They decided to form a new government, one that would leave the power in the hands of Rome's subjects instead of its leaders. And while the early years after Tarquinius' rule were characterized by turmoil and constant battles against neighboring tribes that attempted to prey upon the kingless Romans, eventually, a whole new type of government rose from the darkness. This was the world's first republic.

The republic was governed by two consuls, who were elected for only brief terms—at first, as short as a single year—by the Roman Senate. And for many years, once the republic had been firmly established, it flourished tremendously. This unique form of government proved to forge a city that grew into a nation far more powerful than its neighbors. Despite the tragedy of the sacking of Rome by the Gauls in 390 BCE, leaders rose up not only to defend the city but also to expand its lands until Italy, Macedonia, and parts of Northern Africa fell under Roman command. Back in the city itself, culture began to thrive thanks to contact with the Greeks. In 450 BCE, the Twelve Tables of Roman law were inscribed and put on display in the Roman Forum. Those laws formed the foundation of Western law, and the principles put forth there are still in use to this day.

The republic was far from perfect, despite its great success. Especially in the early years, the patricians, or nobility, were known to suppress the plebeians, or commoners. However, the plebeians continued to push for more power and more say in their fates, and in the later republic, plebeians were able to be elected to high offices, even to the consulship.

The wild success of the Roman Republic proved to be its downfall. Its borders swelled and expanded to encapsulate such a large area that two consuls, lacking absolute power over a vast domain of diverse peoples, struggled to maintain control. In the first century BCE, the Roman consul Sulla became a dictator, which was a role that consuls could take when the republic was under dire duress.

This position came with severe limitations and had to be approved by the Senate, who, in this case, placed Sulla in office with no set time limit. While this had been done before, it had never been done when the republic wasn't in extreme danger. Perhaps Sulla believed that Rome could only survive under the firm control of a harsh leader. However, Sulla's rule was far from what Rome really needed. His people hated him, and from that hatred rose one of Rome's most legendary and famous figures: Julius Caesar.

Caesar was an enemy of Sulla from the start. His marriage to Cornelia, a daughter of one of Sulla's few rivals, caused the angry dictator to attempt to force the young Caesar to divorce his wife. Caesar refused and was exiled for his decision. Even after Cornelia's early death, Caesar could not forget what Sulla had done to him. His strategic and diplomatic skills were sharpened when he was captured by pirates sometime in the 70s BCE, as he succeeded in negotiating his way to freedom—and having the pirates conquered and destroyed.

In the 60s BCE, with Sulla out of the way, consuls ruled over Rome once more—and Caesar was elected to be one of them. He would be the last consul of Rome. Although he would first rule in a triumvirate with two formidable Roman generals, Crassus and Pompey (who had formerly been his most aggressive rivals), Caesar soon found that he was discontent with sharing his power. His military exploits in Gaul and other parts of Europe had expanded Rome's lands considerably, and he wanted them all to himself. With Crassus being handily killed in Parthia, he only had Pompey left to contend with. Jealous of Caesar's power, Pompey tried to assert his dominance over Caesar. The result was disastrous. Caesar famously crossed the Rubicon River and headed straight for Rome, ready to force his power on the city. The ensuing civil war was brutal and one-sided; Pompey was put to flight, and Caesar became the sole ruler of Rome.

He was the first, but he would not be the last. The days of consuls ruling the Roman Republic was over. Rome was about to become something else, something that would prove to be one of Europe's greatest and most enduring powers: The Roman Empire.

Chapter 2 – Born into Turmoil

Julius Caesar was powerful, but like many powerful men, he was also unpopular; in fact, he was so unpopular that in March 44 BCE, a group of senators seized him where he sat at his podium and started driving their knives into his body, harshly and mercilessly. Twenty-three stab wounds later, Julius Caesar was dead. The Roman Republic died with him.

The assassins were men who had been a part of Caesar's inner circle, men who had been intimately involved in the government, and they had grown sick of him. Although Caesar never held the title of emperor, he was known as the *Dictator Perpetuo*—the dictator for life. Fearing that Rome was on a fast track to becoming an absolute monarchy once again, the senators decided that there was only one way out. Despite the fact that Caesar had brought great stability and prosperity to all of his enormous lands, he was deeply hated by the Senate. Their hope was that by killing Julius Caesar, the Roman Republic would be restored once more.

But it was not to be. Before his death, Caesar had nominated his successor, making it clear that he wanted his title to be hereditary instead of allowing the next ruler of Rome to be elected. This successor was his grandnephew, Gaius Julius Caesar, better known by his birth name, Octavian. Octavian had been selected as Caesar's heir when he was still a teenager, and he had been going by the name of Caesar ever since, indicating that he was sure he was destined for great things. Arrogant though it was, he wasn't wrong.

After Caesar's death, the Senate was not united in its determination to see the Roman Republic resurrected. There were several senators who were appalled by the killing of Caesar, as well as supporters of the deceased dictator, and Octavian was quick to ally himself with one of them, a man named Marcus Antonius; or, to give him the name by which Shakespeare immortalized him, Mark Antony. They also reached out to Marcus Aemilius Lepidus, a clergyman who had supported Caesar during his reign, and together, the three of them formed the Second Triumvirate.

Octavian and his friends' rule was not unopposed. In fact, for the first several years of his reign, Octavian would spend most of his time fighting a bloody civil war. With Antony and Lepidus by his side, he set to work fighting against two major enemies: Brutus Cassius, a ringleader of Julius Caesar's assassination, and Sextus Pompeius, the son of Pompey. Ultimately, Octavian, Antony, and Lepidus were successful, but the Second Triumvirate crumbled under the weight of the war. Lepidus was ousted, and Antony and Octavian ruled together.

Unlike Caesar, it appears that Octavian was still quite content to share his power with Mark Antony. Antony was a gifted military commander and an able administrator, but he had one great weakness, and her name was Cleopatra. The beautiful and capable queen of Egypt had captured Antony's heart when he had stayed there during his Parthian campaign, and he had married her, even though Octavian had given him one of his own daughters to wed. Their relationship soured, going further downhill when Antony accused Octavian of not even being the rightful heir to Rome. The Senate was on Octavian's side, and they backed him when a civil war was declared, stripping Antony of his consulship. Rome was ruled by one man again, and this one would grow to call himself emperor.

First, though, he had to contend with Mark Antony. The former consul would not be ousted as easily as Octavian and his Senate had hoped. He had been Caesar's right-hand man when they had charged over the Rubicon and attacked Rome, and he still viewed himself as a loyalist. Cleopatra had captured his heart, but when he handed her some of Rome's Egyptian territories, it had not simply been because she was his lover. It had been because she had been Julius Caesar's lover, too, and she had possibly borne him a son. Although it is not known for certain if this child was actually Caesar's, Antony was certain that the boy was the rightful heir to the imperial title. But he was ready to grab his fair share of power too.

Cleopatra became the villain of the hour, as she was accused of seducing both Caesar and Antony. She was a formidable threat, the queen of an important realm that would be a dangerous enemy to Rome, and Octavian was determined to prove that he could rule as Caesar had. Mustering a 200,000-strong army, led by his favorite general Marcus Agrippa, he set off for Egypt but not before rooting out any semblance of resistance in Rome itself. Anyone who sympathized with Antony was at risk, and Tiberius Claudius Nero was one of those people.

Tiberius Nero was a seasoned military commander in his fifties who had served for longer than Octavian had even been alive. He had first proved his mettle in the 40s BCE, fighting against Pompey and other rivals in the Alexandrian War on the side of Julius Caesar. Tiberius Nero had made a name for himself as a strong commander, being elevated to the title of quaestor, but he quickly began to lose his trust in Caesar. He had old-fashioned values, clinging to the hope that Rome could still be governed as a republic despite its vastness, and when Caesar proved to be more and more of a dictator, Tiberius Nero began to passively resist him. Luckily for him, Tiberius Nero never took action against Caesar, and despite his vociferous support of Caesar's assassins, he was elected as a praetor two years after Caesar's death.

When Octavian proved to follow closely in Caesar's footsteps and the Second Triumvirate crumbled to pieces, Tiberius Nero knew that he couldn't remain neutral. He was terrified of what Octavian's rule would mean for him and his small, but growing, family.

Twenty years ago, Tiberius Nero might have elected to fight against Octavian, but not now. Recently, he had married a beautiful girl named Livia Drusilla—a woman at least two decades his junior who was also his cousin. Livia was enchanting. Beautiful, modest, and quiet, she was the ideal picture of a Roman wife, the perfect understudy for a powerful military leader. She had been only sixteen years old when she had married Tiberius Nero, which was shortly after Caesar was killed, and she had changed the rugged commander's world. Her gentleness stirred his heart away from warfare, and his world shifted even more in 42 BCE, two years after the assassination. It was on November 16th, in a luxurious villa on one of Rome's seven famous hills (the Palatine Hill), that young Livia brought Tiberius Nero's very first child into the world. It was a boy, and what was more, he was a healthy child: a rare gift in an ancient world fraught with disease. Tiberius Nero was delighted. He named the child after himself—Tiberius Claudius Nero. He would be better known simply by his first name: Tiberius.

Despite Tiberius Nero's hopes, Tiberius would not be raised in the peace and sanctuary of the mansion on the Palatine Hill. By 41/40 BCE, Octavian was marching on Mark Antony and Cleopatra, and civil war had divided Rome on a single, jagged line. There was no staying neutral; even the streets were rife with talk over who was going to be the next ruler of Rome. Tiberius Nero could not be exempt from taking sides, even though he appeared to want nothing more than to settle down with his wife and infant son. Tiberius Nero could not bring himself to trust Octavian. There was something treacherous about the ruler, something he couldn't depend on. He chose to ally himself with Mark Antony instead, and so, he had no choice but to flee Rome with his wife and two-year-old little Tiberius.

For Tiberius Nero, this meant shattering his dreams. For Livia, it meant being catapulted from a life of relative security and luxury into a terrifying series of flights from one attacker after the other. And for little Tiberius, a mere toddler, it meant a hard childhood with implications that would stay with him forever.

Chapter 3 – The Eye of the Emperor

Tiberius Claudius Nero the younger's first memories were all about running.

On the coast of Egypt, Octavian was wreaking havoc upon Mark Antony's forces, striking him with one defeat after the other. Each defeat spelled greater disaster for Antony's supporters, including Tiberius Nero and Livia. Livia was little more than a frightened child herself, a teenage girl with a baby in her arms; she had nothing to rely on other than her husband's ability to keep them out of harm's way. Fleeing farther and farther east, Tiberius Nero took them from Sicily to Greece, avoiding disaster by the skin of his teeth at every turn.

But little Tiberius knew nothing of civil wars and angry emperors. All he was aware of was the fact that his life was ever-changing. They would be settled down in one home, and just as he started to get used to it, his mother would wake him in the night, tuck him into her arms, and flee into the darkness on her husband's heels, admonishing young Tiberius over and over to be quiet. He heard the battle cries sometimes as the war caused unrest throughout the empire. And little Tiberius, clinging to his mother's dress, was terrified.

It was no way for a child to live. But live he would, as Tiberius Nero managed to keep them one step ahead of their enemies.

* * * *

Just months after beginning his affair with Cleopatra, Mark Antony would return to the fold, even though he was much older than the youthful Octavian. The younger consul's forces had wreaked havoc on Antony's, forcing him to return even though his heart still longed for the queen who had seduced him. Antony had little choice other than to marry Octavian's sister, Octavia the Younger, and settle down, ending the civil war around 40 BCE.

But this peace was short-lived. Antony loved Cleopatra too passionately and was too desperate to hold his own power, and he wouldn't allow himself to be pushed around by a young upstart like Octavian for long. In 37 BCE, he returned to Egypt and Cleopatra. They both became heroes and gods in the eyes of the people they served, and Cleopatra supported her Roman husband during the Roman-Parthian Wars that still raged in modern-day Turkey and Iran. By 32 BCE, Antony had regained his confidence. He separated from Octavia the Younger, and war was declared once again between Antony in the east and Octavian in the west.

This time, however, Octavian was ready. He had established himself as the sole ruler of his part of the Roman state, and he was ready to seize the whole thing for himself. Summoning an army hundreds of thousands strong, Octavian attacked at Actium on September 2nd, 31 BCE. In a heated naval battle, brilliantly commanded by Agrippa, Octavian put Cleopatra and Antony both to flight. They returned to the city of Alexandria, where Antony, knowing he was beaten, committed suicide in Cleopatra's own mausoleum. Cleopatra clung to life a few days longer, but when she realized that Octavian was the one Roman ruler that could resist her seduction, she followed suit.

With that, Rome and its lands were united once more. And Octavian returned to his capital city, utterly unrivaled.

* * * *

It was during the first peace between Octavian and Antony, around 40 BCE, that amnesty was granted to all the enemies of Octavian during the civil war. For thousands of people across the empire, it was a much-needed sigh of relief. For Tiberius Nero and Livia, it was like the end of a bad dream. Tiberius Nero could finally return to the city he loved and his home on the Palatine Hill to raise his little boy and care for his pregnant wife in the peace that he longed for.

Sadly, for the family, returning to Rome proved to be a catastrophic choice. They would have been better off had they stayed safely in Greece, far away from Octavian's wandering eyes. Not that Octavian was an enemy of the family by the time they had returned to Rome. Instead, he would prove to be far too friendly.

Livia was now a young woman in the full bloom of her beauty. Around twenty years old at the time, she was absolutely striking; with flawless pale skin and bright, soulful eyes, she turned heads when she walked down the street, especially next to her grizzled old husband. Not only was she beautiful and gentle—and obviously fertile, having three-year-old Tiberius close at her heels—but she was also part of a prominent family. The way she bore herself was regal, with a timeless dignity that spoke to the sentiment of the people about the old Roman Republic. Added to that, despite her innocent, guileless eyes, Livia was fiercely intelligent. To Octavian, who would soon divorce his second wife in 38 BCE, she checked all the boxes.

Tiberius didn't know of these things, of course. As he spent two years of happy childhood getting the best of everything on the

Palatine Hill, all he knew was that Livia was his mother, and he loved her. To all appearances, Livia and Tiberius Nero's marriage remained solid, despite the fact that Tiberius Nero was so much older than she was. Love and laughter, for a time, echoed through the walls of the villa as Livia's belly began to swell with the promise of Tiberius Nero's second child.

It all fell apart in 37 BCE when Octavian finally made his move. He wanted Livia, and the fact that she was a wife and mother would not deter him. He demanded that Livia marry him, and therefore, she would have to divorce Tiberius Nero. It's unclear how exactly Octavian made this happen, but it's abundantly clear that Tiberius Nero could not say no to the most powerful man in the Western world. With a heavy heart, he let his young wife go—and Tiberius had to watch his mother leave.

Overnight, Tiberius' world fell to pieces. The house on the Palatine Hill was suddenly very quiet, its stately pillars now as silent as gravestones, casting their long shadows over a cold and empty home.

Chapter 4 – In the Shadow of Augustus

The young woman, dressed in off-white muslin, walked slowly, the soft fabric draping down almost to the floor. The yellow flammeum—a veil that enclosed her head but kept her face open—was not enough to hide her red-rimmed eyes. This was not the first marriage ceremony that she would take part in. It was all familiar to her: the complicated knot holding the strip of wool that served as her belt, the intricate style in which her hair was pinned up and adorned with flowers. Even the steady pressure on her arm of the older man taking every step beside her was familiar.

Except, this time, Livia Drusilla was not walking beside her own father. She was walking down the aisle with Tiberius Nero, the man that she had grown to love. Despite the fact that they looked more like father and daughter than husband and wife, Livia had followed him to the very ends of her world. She had given birth to his children. She had had happy times with him, and those times were now at an end. Tiberius Nero was now her ex-husband, and she was walking beside him for the last time.

Octavian waited to receive her, beaming at the beautiful prize that he had wrested from Tiberius Nero's grip. The old commander gave her away, both literally and figuratively, going with her to the very end. And with that simple gesture, he ripped young Tiberius' world in half.

* * * *

When Livia married Octavian, she was likely heavily pregnant with Tiberius Nero's child. It was just weeks later that she brought the baby into the world, and it was another little boy, strong and healthy like his brother. But unlike Tiberius, this little one would not be allowed to experience the embrace of his mother's arms. It is debated whether he was born directly before or directly after the marriage, but either way, the result was the same. The baby, named Drusus Claudius Nero after Livia's late father, was stripped away from her far too soon. He was sent to live back on the Palatine Hill with his father and older brother, Tiberius.

Baby Drusus, of course, could hardly have known what was really happening to him; a man of Tiberius Nero's means would have quickly secured a reliable nurse to care for the child. But to Tiberius, the world had become terrible and confusing. He was only about five or six years old, a child that was deeply attached to his mother, but now she was gone. For three long years, Tiberius would live with his baby brother, seeing his mother only now and then in passing parades and public appearances. She had become Rome's crown jewel, but to Tiberius, she still just looked like his mother.

Little did Tiberius know that he would soon lose even more than his mother. His father, alone and aging, his military career ended in ignominy, his beautiful young wife brutally taken from him, would not live much longer.

* * * *

Tiberius' short legs were already exhausted from bringing up the rear of the long procession. Just walking a long distance through the streets of Rome was a tall order for any little boy of nine; doing it at the rear of his own father's funeral procession was almost impossible. The professional mourners had led the way so Tiberius couldn't see much of them from his spot at the back, but he could hear them shrieking as they ripped out their hair and dragged their fingernails across their faces. They would have been followed by actors representing Tiberius Nero's ancestors, and then there would have been the bier, where Tiberius Nero's body lay. Tiberius couldn't really believe that the pale, rigid thing lying on the bier was really his father. The Tiberius Nero he'd known had laughed and cried and taught him and Drusus lessons and disciplined them for being rude. But this Tiberius Nero was stiff and cold.

Tiberius and Drusus, along with other more distant members of Tiberius Nero's family, brought up the rear. Drusus was only three. Perhaps Tiberius was jealous of him, knowing that he didn't hold the weighty responsibility of being the older brother, of having to perform the sacred duty that awaited him.

Once the procession was over, Tiberius Nero's body was taken to the necropolis to be cremated. The adults had told Tiberius that when the burning happened, Tiberius Nero's shade would cross the Styx, and he would enter the afterlife. Tiberius wasn't sure what the afterlife was like, but he knew that nobody ever came back.

He also knew that the next part of the funeral—the eulogy—was his final duty to his dead father. Despite being only nine, Tiberius would be the one to deliver the lengthy eulogy for his father. Tiberius Nero had paid for his boys to have a good education, and it paid off. Tiberius made it through the eulogy, his first public appearance.

And then his life changed again forever. With their father gone, Tiberius and Drusus had to go and live with their mother, Livia, and her husband, the ruler of Rome.

* * * *

Upon his return from the war with Antony and Cleopatra in 31 BCE, two years after Tiberius first came to live with him, Octavian knew that he was ready to become the sole ruler of Rome. But Julius Caesar's assassination had taught him a harsh lesson. If he was going to become Rome's first emperor, he had to do it more slowly, exercising more tact. Thus, he had a second consul elected: Marcus Agrippa, the commander who had brought him victory over Antony.

It was still evident that Octavian was looking for more power than any Roman ruler had held before, but his diplomacy was paying off. Despite being the richest man in the empire, and undoubtedly holding far more power than the Senate thanks to his careful political moves, Octavian was well-liked. This was proven in January 27 BCE when the Senate chose to bestow upon him a title that no Roman had borne before: Augustus. It means "illustrious" and holds an almost divine connotation, and Octavian loved it. While he served alongside some other consuls in the next few years, it was evident that Octavian was now the sole ruler of Rome, and 27 BCE is traditionally viewed as the end of the Roman Republic and the start of the Roman Empire.

Meanwhile, Octavian was already flirting with the idea of appointing an heir. He favored his nephew, a young man named Marcus Claudius Marcellus, since his marriage to Livia had been unproductive.

Tiberius, now a boy of fifteen, was not treated badly in the palace of Augustus. It is easy to imagine that the teenager must have struggled with living in the house of the man who took his mother away, the man who broke his father's heart. However, Tiberius and Drusus were both supplied with the best of everything. Augustus spared no expense in their education, and they were raised alongside Marcellus, knowing that their noble birth and high education would likely give them important positions in the empire one day.

Shortly after receiving the title of Augustus, the rising emperor headed to the war front in Gaul. Germanic tribes there were still resisting the Romans, and Augustus had two reasons for inspecting the border: firstly, to check that his empire was in no danger, and secondly, to expose his prospective heir to battle. He took Marcellus with him, and Tiberius tagged along too. It was not the first time that Tiberius would feel the tension of war and hear the clash and cry of battle; he had heard it in the distance when he was just a toddler as his parents tried to stay away from Octavian. This time, he was riding through it at the heel of the man from whom he and his family had fled for years in his earliest memories.

Difficult as Tiberius' teenage years must have been emotionally, his life would soon take a turn for the better—and strangely enough, his fortune was due to a tragedy. The trip to the front lines had shown Marcellus to be a promising commander and soldier, making Augustus even more certain of his choice of heir. Augustus did have one child, though: Julia, a young girl who had been born a little more than a year before he married Livia. In fact, Julia was the only reason he had waited as long as he did to divorce his second wife, Scribonia. He actually divorced Scribonia the same day Julia was born.

Julia had grown up in the household of a woman who wasn't her mother, and it had made her difficult and bitter. However, she was still of strategic importance to the empire. Augustus took advantage of this by betrothing her to Marcellus, strengthening his position as heir, even though Julia was just twelve years old. She was little more than a pawn to Augustus, but at least she was betrothed to a boy she knew, a boy she'd grown up with and who was closer to her own age. Marcellus had been born in the same year as Tiberius, making him three years older than Julia. They married in 25 BCE.

Just two years later, tragedy struck. Marcellus died. Augustus and the empire were thrown into a panic; the young man, nineteen at the time of his death, had been instrumental in the future of Rome. Augustus was forced to turn to his most loyal ally, Agrippa, who was then in his forties. To Julia's absolute horror, she was promptly married off to the old general in 21 BCE, even though she was nearly 25 years his junior. Unlike the relatively peaceful union of Livia and Tiberius Nero, this marriage was not a happy one.

For Tiberius, however, it proved to be a boon, because when Agrippa came to the palace, he brought someone with him—someone beautiful and sweet and gentle, a mere girl of fifteen years old with alluring eyes that captured Tiberius' heart at once. She was Agrippa's daughter, Vipsania Agrippina. And within a few weeks, Tiberius was hopelessly, madly, insanely in love with her.

Chapter 5 – First Conquest

Illustration I: A first-century statue of Tiberius from Paestum.

Vipsania changed Tiberius' world from the moment that she walked into it.

Sources differ on whether Tiberius and Vipsania had been betrothed since Vipsania was a baby and when Tiberius had just been adopted into Augustus' family. It is plausible, considering that Augustus was looking to create multiple options for successors in the event of his death. Either way, it is quite clear that Vipsania and Tiberius fell wildly in love—and that, whether it was arranged or not, Tiberius was eager to get married to the wide-eyed young girl who had so intensely captured his restless heart.

It would appear that all the bitterness of his youth had begun to melt away for Tiberius every time Vipsania's eyes shone sunlight into his heart. They wasted little time in getting married. In 20 BCE, shortly after the union of Julia and Agrippa, Tiberius and Vipsania were married.

After his tumultuous childhood, things were finally beginning to look up for Tiberius, who was 22 years old by this time. He was still stuck with his stepfather, whom he probably still hated, but at least his nearness to Augustus was enabling him to attain higher and higher ranks. Marcellus' death had made Tiberius and Drusus both potential heirs to the imperial throne, as Agrippa was too old, and he and Julia had yet to produce grandchildren for Augustus. In 24 BCE, Tiberius had been elected to the rank of quaestor, and so, he entered the world of politics. It proved to be a world that he grew to love; he became an advocate, and in a world where law was still in its infancy, and the roles of judges and advocates were more about arguing rhetoric, he found it nonetheless stimulating.

Tiberius and Vipsania hadn't been married for long when he was called to the front, this time to a far more pressing military matter than just checking up on some military outposts. Armenia, a richly abundant country that was particularly well known for its endless supply of good chariot horses, had been captured by one of Rome's greatest enemies: Parthia. Armenia itself had been a battleground for generals as legendary as Crassus, Pompey, and even Mark Antony. It had been under Parthian control for some time while Augustus focused on sorting out his own civil war, but when a group of

Roman sympathizers assassinated the Armenian king—who had been little more than a figurehead of Parthian control—Augustus knew it was time to take action. And who better to send to the front than his twenty-something potential heir, Tiberius?

Tiberius headed out to the front in 20 BCE alongside a young Armenian royal named Tigranes, and they reached Armenia in time to launch a massive campaign, which was massively successful. Helped by the Roman sympathizers within Armenia, Tiberius and Tigranes were able to defeat the Parthians. Tiberius installed Tigranes on the throne, where he was crowned Tigranes III of Armenia, and ushered in a seventy-year-long treaty with Parthia that would keep a kind of peace that Armenia and Rome both desperately needed.

Returning to Rome, Tiberius was hailed as a hero by adoring crowds, soldiers who respected his even-handed treatment of his troops, a proud emperor, and a beautiful doe-eyed wife. He was given a glorious triumph through the city, a parade to honor and exalt his accomplishments. Riding in a chariot drawn by white horses, with a purple cloak thrown over his shoulders, Tiberius was arm in arm with the beautiful woman whom he adored. The crowds of Rome cheered wildly as Vipsania giggled by his side, and life had never been better for the victorious young praetor.

Yet in just a few short years, life would take an appalling turn for the worse.

Chapter 6 – Forced Marriage

By 18 BCE, Rome itself was entering a period of stability. The civil war had long been dealt with; there were, as always, a few rebellious factions messing around in Gaul, but nothing to threaten the empire itself. Even Parthia had finally been subdued for a while. Best of all, despite Julia's steady hatred of her aging husband, she had managed to bear two boys to Agrippa. Gaius Caesar and Lucius Caesar were healthy boys, grandsons of Augustus, and as such, they were perfect heirs to the Roman Empire. Augustus had adopted them both as his own, and he was clearly set to groom them to succeed him.

For Tiberius, this meant that he was quite low on the list of potential heirs to the throne, but he was not particularly concerned at that point. He was newly married to a beautiful woman, enjoying a career in politics that he loved, even though it was unlikely to make him an emperor, and a successful, well-respected man of war. Life was good.

In 16 BCE, Tiberius and his brother Drusus were once again sent off to the battlefield. It was still a blow to Tiberius to leave Vipsania behind, but he was ready to face battle once again. This time, he left for modern-day Austria, Switzerland, and Bavaria. Germanic tribes were causing scuffles with Roman troops there, and Tiberius and his brother were sent to subdue them.

The landscape of those countries, which is so civilized and manicured today, was still almost completely wild and undocumented at the time. The tribes that lived there, though formidable in battle, were not as dedicated to order and literature as the Romans. Tiberius saw them as barbarians, and their country was beautiful but untamed. Their tribes, though they fought like demons, were also fairly easily defeated by Tiberius' legions. Instead of spending all his time in hard fighting, Tiberius was able to explore the magnificent country; particularly, he started to follow the course of the Danube River. The second-longest river in Europe, its winding length runs for nearly two thousand miles across the continent, spanning ten countries. Even in ancient times, it was rich in natural resources and served as an important trade route. Tiberius was able to track it, covering long miles with the help of horses, all the way to its source. Hidden deep in the hostile territory of modern-day Germany, then known as Gaul, Tiberius found the place where the mighty Danube sprang up from the earth, as fresh as water can possibly be. Today, the source is known as the Donauquelle, and the spring is surrounded by marble pillars and an imperious sculpture of a beautiful young woman and plump little cherubs. Then, it was just a rich stream of the purest water welling up in the midst of the German wilderness, but it was equally impressive. Just as impressive was the fact that, having fought his way up the Danube, Tiberius had established the reaches of the Roman Empire all the way into northern Germany.

Returning home once more in triumph in 15 BCE, Tiberius was elevated to the rank of consul, as Gaius and Lucius were still far too young to hold any kind of political title. Even though consuls did not hold the same power as they once had—Augustus was now undoubtedly the sole ruler of the empire, even though he did not actually refer to himself as emperor—it was still an impressive rank, and Tiberius and Vipsania settled down to three years of peace, prosperity, and prominence in Rome.

But it did not last forever. In 12 BCE, Agrippa died. His death was a terrible blow to Augustus and to the Roman Empire. Augustus had grown up alongside Agrippa; they had been friends, comrades, even family. Worse, Agrippa had been Augustus' trusted adviser and supporter—and the husband of Julia. His death was disastrous, and it left Julia unmarried. With Marcellus long dead and Agrippa's sons Gaius and Lucius mere boys, there was only one man left who could take the throne now, and that man was Tiberius.

Tiberius was a hero, but he was only a stepson to Augustus (via Livia, who was not well-liked by the public), and the emperor knew that he would have to solidify their family ties in order for Tiberius to be accepted as a successor in the event of Augustus' death. So, he did to Tiberius exactly what he had done to Tiberius' father.

He forced him to divorce the woman that he adored.

The blow came out of nowhere, shattering Tiberius' happy world. Just as he had finally come to grips with the life into which Augustus had catapulted him, just when things were looking up for him at last, Tiberius was about to lose the thing he loved most. Of course, marriage with Julia would give him even more social prominence, the promise even of becoming the emperor of Rome one day. But compared to losing Vipsania, that honor was nothing to him. Tiberius didn't want to be emperor. He wanted to be Vipsania's husband, but just like Tiberius Nero, he knew he couldn't argue.

To make matters even worse, Tiberius would be forced to marry Julia, a woman who was hated through the length and breadth of the empire. Julia's beauty was equaled only by her extravagance. Spoiled as a child but bullied into marrying one man after the other as an adult, Julia was only 27 years old and had already gone through two husbands. Being married off to a third only served to deepen her bitterness. She had borne three children to a man she did not love at first and was pregnant with a fourth; she had been dragged all over the empire as Agrippa's duties took him from Gaul to Judea and back again. To make matters worse, it would appear that Julia's heart had even begun to soften toward Agrippa, despite the fact that she had a reputation of being unfaithful toward him early in their marriage. Just as she finally began to love him, Agrippa had died, and now she had to marry Tiberius. They had grown up in the same household, and it must have felt like marrying a brother. Perhaps she harbored some resentment toward Tiberius since she had grown up groomed to be a princess that would be handed out to the most eligible husband, while Tiberius had the freedom to make war and be a consul and do so much more than she ever could.

Julia had been betrothed to the son of Mark Antony when she was only two years old. From that day onward, although the marriage was never realized thanks to the civil war, her life had been relentlessly controlled by her father. She was not allowed to see or speak to anyone unless he had approved them already; she couldn't play in the street like the plebeian children. Confined to her room, she sought solace in books and education, and now with Agrippa dead and both her boys adopted to Augustus' household, they were all she had left.

Tiberius had no choice. He said his final goodbye to Vipsania, whom he still adored, knowing that there was no other way. He had been only three years old when Livia had dragged him through the night, fleeing from the battle cries and the smoke, running away from Octavian when war broke out with Antony. Tiberius was a grown man now, a consul, far more powerful than Tiberius Nero had ever been. But just like when he was a toddler, Augustus still decided what his fate would be.

And his fate was to marry Julia. He did so, reluctantly and quickly, and as soon as possible after the wedding, Tiberius fled back to the battlefield in the company of his brother and only remaining friend, Drusus. Even the warlike Germanic tribes could not compare to the sharp-tongued, bitter, mourning princess that had become his wife.

Chapter 7 – Rock Bottom

Illustration II: A 17th-century engraving of Vipsania

Drusus was dead.

Tiberius had been there, but it was too late. He had held his brother's hand, watching as the once-mighty general and governor of Gaul slipped slowly from this world, comatose and helpless and a long,

long way from home. Tiberius could do nothing to save him, just as he had been unable to do anything to prevent Vipsania from being torn from his arms or to keep his family together when he was only a boy and Augustus took his mother from him. Now, he watched his baby brother die, slowly and in pain.

It was not a battle that took Drusus' life, even though he had been at war for most of his years. By all accounts, Drusus was a skilled and intelligent general—but he was also fearless and occasionally a little extravagant with his personal skills in battle. Detesting Augustus from the start, Drusus left Rome at the earliest opportunity and stayed away for as long as he could. He had been in Italy just long enough to marry Augustus' niece, Antonia Minor, who was also the daughter of Mark Antony. As much as he hated Augustus, he deeply and powerfully loved Antonia, remaining ceaselessly faithful to her. She was waiting in his new home, Lugdunum (modern-day Lyon, France), with his young children, waiting for a husband that would never come home.

Just like Tiberius was waiting for a brother that would never wake up.

Drusus had been at war with the Germanic tribes for most of his adult life, and he had won several outstanding victories. He had conquered entirely new territories, expanding the borders of Rome and adding Germanic kings as tributaries. Yet it was not a battle that killed him. It was an accident—a simple, silly accident, a fall from a horse. He clung to life for a month after the fall, during which time Tiberius, who had been riding to meet him with an eye to conquer some tribes and soothe his wounded heart after the loss of Vipsania, arrived by his dying brother's side. There would be no conquering; there would be only heartache. Drusus had been well-loved, especially by Tiberius and by Antonia, who lived out the next fifty years of her life without remarrying—as faithful as Drusus had been in his life, so was Antonia faithful after his death.

Tiberius' grief was tremendous. He needed the whole world to know how deeply he had loved his last friend in the world, and so, he walked back to Rome, a distance of more than a thousand miles. It would have taken months. He declined to ride a horse when his brother's body was lying in a wagon and arrived back in Rome around 9/8 BCE.

With Drusus gone, Tiberius' only close family left was his mother, his young son by Vipsania, and Julia. Livia was happily causing intrigue and chaos, perhaps as a kind of revenge for being stolen away from her life with Tiberius Nero (rumor had it that she wanted to put one of her sons on the imperial throne, and her attempts to do so were causing scandal); Tiberius' son, Drusus (named after Tiberius' brother instead of his father, which was uncommon during this time), had been packed off with his mother; Julia had fallen into drunkenness in Tiberius' absence, and she was perhaps even then already engaged in a secret affair. However, she and Tiberius must have drawn at least slightly closer because, in 6 BCE, she gave birth to a son. The boy did not last long enough for history to know his name. He died as a baby, and Tiberius felt robbed.

Stumbling through the streets, trying to carry out the duties that he now carried as a Roman tribune, Tiberius was half-blinded in a cloud of grief and depression when he saw her. Vipsania. She hadn't noticed his presence; she had remarried, of course, to a prominent senator named Gaius Asinius Gallus Saloninus, a man that Tiberius hated passionately, not least because Gallus claimed that Drusus—Tiberius' son by Vipsania—was his own son. Vipsania was just walking through the streets, and she was a symbol of everything that Tiberius had lost. He could not contain himself. He stumbled after her, crying openly, the terrible sound of his grief echoing from building to building, his unashamed weeping so loud that it was the physical manifestation of a man who had lost everything he once loved.

It would be the last time that Tiberius loved anything with all of his heart.

* * * *

To rub salt into the wound, around 5 BCE—close to the time when Tiberius saw Vipsania again—Augustus' biological grandson and adopted son, Gaius Caesar, turned fifteen. Relieved that a biological heir had made it to a relatively mature age, Augustus began to shower all of his attention on young Gaius, who had never taken up a sword to defend or expand the empire but was lucky enough to be born with the right DNA. Tiberius, once so close to being heir to the Roman throne, was practically forgotten. Once again, he was nothing but a pawn in Augustus' ruthless game.

Abruptly, Tiberius had had enough. He could no longer stand living under Augustus' shadow. Drusus' last campaign had been so successful that Augustus had even closed the doors of the temple of Janus, the Roman god of war, signifying total peace in the empire. There were no barbarians to suppress in order to give Tiberius a purpose anymore. Julia was being extravagantly awful; she stumbled around drunk in public and brought shame to Tiberius. After the embarrassing spectacle that Tiberius had caused when he saw Vipsania, Augustus had even forbidden him from seeing her again.

Sick of it all, Tiberius simply gave up. He retired from politics and moved to the Greek island of Rhodes, a tropical paradise where he was able to live in comfort—and far away from prying Roman eyes and the humiliating gossip that constantly surrounded Julia. Maybe, out here, far from Augustus, Tiberius could finally live his own life in freedom. Tragically, it would appear that he did no such thing. Instead, depressed, Tiberius quietly withdrew from society and from his duties. He spent his time alone, having no one left in the world that he truly loved, his heart broken and embittered.

Soon, even Julia would no longer be with him. In 2 BCE, she succeeded in causing a terrible scandal when her illicit relationship with a noble-blooded man named Iullus Antonius came to light. There was more to the story than a simple extramarital affair, although it's unclear how much of the tales surrounding Julia's promiscuity are true. Several men were executed or forced to commit suicide, possibly as a result of relationships with Julia. As for Julia herself, Augustus—worried for the future of the empire and sick of her nonsense—had her sent in exile to the island of Pandateria (modern-day Ventotene). She was accompanied only by her mother, Scribonia, and forbidden to have any visitors at all. Considering that Pandateria was almost uninhabited, it was nothing short of torture for the social Julia.

For Tiberius, at least, his wife's exile was a boon. And another boon was coming, or perhaps it better be called a curse. Tiberius would soon be the only living heir to the imperial throne.

Chapter 8 – Ascension

Despite the fact that Augustus had clearly started grooming Gaius for his heir and pushed Tiberius to the side, he was appalled by his stepson's abrupt move to Rhodes just as his career in Rome was looking promising. Gaius was obviously his favorite, but Augustus was no fool. He knew how quickly things could change, and Tiberius was still his backup plan. He implored Tiberius to return to Rome. Tiberius, however, steadfastly refused. He had spent his life at the beck and call of the Roman emperor. He was not about to come home like a good boy now.

According to one tale—its truth is somewhat disputed—Augustus decided to pretend that he was terribly ill. This ruse finally got Tiberius' attention. Not for Augustus' sake, but for that of the empire for which he had fought so hard, Tiberius sailed from Rhodes. He did not set foot in Rome, however. Instead, he anchored not far from the city, waiting for word. When Augustus finally gave up and made a miraculous recovery, Tiberius turned right back around and sailed home to his island paradise. With that, Tiberius' retirement was no longer simply a retirement. Augustus was outraged that, after years of meekly following his orders, Tiberius would commit this act of rebellion. Even when Tiberius felt guilty about his actions and would have returned to Rome to help, Augustus refused, and with that, Tiberius was in exile.

Writing Tiberius off effortlessly, Augustus turned his attention to his adopted sons. It was about 2 BCE when he started to give Lucius, now a late teenager, just as much attention as he had given Gaius. The boys were both young men now, and Augustus felt confident that they would be able to succeed him. Let Tiberius mope in Rhodes; Augustus didn't need him.

It was not to be.

Tiberius had just accepted his fate of living in solitude, trying his best to avoid his own wife, when disaster struck in 2 CE: Lucius, the younger of Augustus' two adopted sons, died. Augustus, knowing that he was running out of heirs, had no choice but to permit Tiberius' return to Rome in case something happened to his last remaining biological heir, Gaius. And in 4 CE, something did happen. Gaius had been sent to Armenia to sort out an uprising in the area—he was a twenty-something young man by now, well educated, and a capable consul—when he was wounded in the thick of the fighting. The wounds proved to be fatal, and just like that, the fate of the Roman Empire was suddenly and precariously hanging in the balance.

Augustus was 67 by this time, and he knew that he wasn't going to live forever. He had to act fast to secure the future of the empire, and Tiberius was all that he had left. Tiberius must have been well aware that he was a fourth or fifth choice to be Augustus' successor, but he allowed himself to be briskly adopted as Augustus' son and hastily groomed to become the next Roman emperor. Either way, with Julia out of his life, Tiberius seems to have started doing better. He was sent to the Germanic front once again in 9 CE to defeat a batch of tribes that had been causing considerable trouble for the Roman legions there, and his mission was greatly successful.

The people had started to put their faith in Tiberius again, which was a good thing because only five years later —in 14 CE and at the ripe age of 77—Augustus Caesar, the first emperor of Rome, died of natural causes. Even in his death, he controlled Tiberius' fate by passing the Roman Empire on to him. At the age of 56, Tiberius, worn down and embittered by a life of harassment from the late emperor, was now an emperor himself.

Chapter 9 – A Slippery Slope to Capri

Illustration III: Roman coinage bearing Tiberius' image. Tiberius was Emperor of Rome at the time of Jesus Christ, and the coin mentioned in the Gospels was likely identical to those pictured.

The first few years of Tiberius' reign were promising.

Augustus had been ruling over Rome for a long and largely peaceful period; while there had been trouble in Gaul and Armenia, once the civil war with Mark Antony was over, the Romans living in Italy and Rome itself had enjoyed prosperity and stability. There was some trepidation about Tiberius taking the throne at first, particularly from the armies, who supported a man named Germanicus Julius Caesar Claudianus, the late Drusus' son, thus Tiberius' nephew. Germanicus was a skilled general and the husband of Agrippina the Elder, one of Agrippa and Julia's daughters, which gave him a familial link to Augustus. Germanicus could likely have landed Tiberius into plenty of hot water if he had chosen to rebel against the new emperor. At Augustus' request, Tiberius adopted Germanicus as his son, and probably to his surprise, Germanicus proved to be wholeheartedly supportive of his adoptive father. He was a stalwart friend and loyal to a fault, and for the first time since Drusus died, Tiberius felt like he had a family again.

With Germanicus taking care of the military side of things, and stability returning to Tiberius' home life, he was free to focus on his rule. His mother, Livia, was determined to meddle as much as possible, trying rule through her son, but Tiberius was able to keep her out of his business, at least at first. He gained a reputation for being modest and moderate, managing Rome's finances well. He even put an end to the lavish gladiatorial games, as Rome's nobility enjoyed them when they should have been paying attention to affairs of state.

For five years, Rome enjoyed a steady peace under an emperor who, while not as extravagantly brilliant as Augustus, was nonetheless a wise and capable administrator. It is perhaps worth noting that, even though he was now the most powerful man in the world, Tiberius failed to force Gallus to divorce Vipsania. Instead, he allowed his ex-wife to enjoy the life that she had been living for decades and turned to governing his empire as well as he could.

It was yet another personal tragedy that would swing Tiberius' reign from excellent to appalling. This man had lost everything—first his mother, then his father, his brother, his wife, his children—and now he was about to lose his adoptive son, too.

Germanicus had continued to be everything that an heir to the empire was expected to be: successful in war, capable in peace, constantly loyal to the emperor, and fertile—abundantly so. In 17 CE, having successfully conquered still more of the Germanic regions, Germanicus was given a triumph and paraded through the streets of Rome alongside his five children. Among those children was a little boy, then named Gaius, who would one day be known as Caligula, a notorious Roman emperor.

Two years later, Germanicus left to tour the Mediterranean and then Egypt. In Egypt—the source of most of the empire's grain—he lowered the price of grain without consulting Tiberius. As much as Tiberius loved the young prince, he was forced to rebuke him, and Germanicus returned to Antioch in Syria on his way back to Rome. Tragically, Tiberius would never see him again. Germanicus died in Antioch in 19 CE, likely poisoned by Piso, a jealous governor who saw him as a rival.

Germanicus' death was a horrific blow to Tiberius' already delicate psyche, and to make matters even worse, the suspicious circumstances of his death quickly turned into a political scandal that spiraled out of control. Agrippina accused Tiberius of having poisoned Germanicus. Tiberius had done no such thing, but his rebuke of the prince lent credibility to Agrippina's story, and her entire family was involved in a long and messy court case. Grieving and distrusted by his people, Tiberius' heart was broken. Agrippina and her second-to-oldest son, Drusus Caesar, were sent into exile, where they both starved to death. One of his other sons, Nero Julius Caesar Germanicus, was eventually assassinated.

The only surviving son of Germanicus was a little boy named Gaius, who only survived because he was deemed to be too young to be a threat to the throne. Tiberius was once again entirely alone, so he latched onto little Gaius, adopting him as his son. With Germanicus gone, Tiberius was vulnerable and soon found himself under attack. Livia was more successful now in meddling in the affairs of the empire; it was possibly with her influence that Tiberius made a terrible blunder in instating a policy known as delation. This was the process by which anyone could make an accusation against an upper-class family. The accusation would usually be punished by confiscating all or part of their wealth, which would then be at least partially dispensed to the accuser. Of course, false accusations followed, and Rome's nobility was quickly and thoroughly turned against Tiberius.

By 26 CE, now rapidly approaching his seventies, Tiberius could no longer deal with the rigors of running the empire. He had increasingly left the Senate alone with the administration, and finally, he decided to simply leave Rome altogether, longing for the peace that he had experienced at Rhodes. He took little Gaius off to the island of Capri and retired there, leaving the empire in the hands of a man named Lucius Aelius Sejanus, a captain of the Praetorian Guard. Sejanus gleefully took all of the power that Tiberius bestowed upon him, and the emperor himself almost entirely withdrew from politics, although he retained his title.

Chapter 10 – The Last Javelin

In his long and weary life, Tiberius had tried time and time again to find fulfillment in his relationships: with Drusus, with Vipsania, with Germanicus. Now, robbed of those he loved, his heart broken more times than he could bear, Tiberius turned to other things to bring him pleasure. And the Villa Jovis on the island of Capri was filled with the worldly pleasures in which the aging emperor chose to indulge.

Villa Jovis stood at the top of a towering cliff, dropping away into the almost impossibly blue waters of the Mediterranean. Its grandiose multiple stories housed a variety of almost unspeakable sexual pleasures. Tiberius had been a warrior, a lover, an emperor; now, he was little more than a nasty old man, seeking for bodily pleasure, his high intellect descended into a pit of madness and lust. And it was in this environment that little Gaius had to grow up, his young mind and eyes exposed to lavish and inappropriate pleasures at a tender age. Considering this, it is little wonder that the boy grew up into the famously mad emperor Caligula.

Tiberius had slipped away into utter depravity, constantly indulging in drinking and sex of every conceivable type. He'd become a drunk and a pervert, but he was still the emperor, and like it or not, he was still responsible for the empire. Sejanus, it would turn out, was a terrible replacement.

It was once again family drama, rather than political threats, that would cause disaster in Rome. Vipsania's son by Tiberius, Drusus, had married a beautiful young woman named Livilla. Sadly, Livilla was more like Julia than like Drusus' mother. She started having an affair with Sejanus, who eventually had Drusus poisoned. When news of his son's death reached Tiberius, he awoke from his stupor for long enough to realize that Sejanus must have killed him. Thus, when Sejanus and Livilla asked Tiberius for permission to marry, the emperor flatly refused. Sejanus was outraged that the man who had dumped the responsibility of a whole empire on his shoulders would dare to refuse his wishes. He and Livilla began a plot against Tiberius, and it was only thanks to a warning from Livilla's mother that the plot was unsuccessful. Tiberius rallied, took himself back to Rome, and had Sejanus and Livilla both horribly executed in 31 CE.

Afterward, Tiberius withdrew once again to Capri, making little to no effort to secure the succession and abandoning the empire to the government of the Senate. Gaius, now a young man named Caligula, was made a quaestor; however, he had not really received the education befitting the heir to the imperial throne. Tiberius, at this point, could no longer be bothered. He had suffered too much. He just wanted to die in peace in Capri, doing whatever he wanted.

Even that would be denied to the lecherous old emperor.

In March of 37 CE, Tiberius had traveled to Misenum, an ancient port of Italy, in order to take part in a ceremony. He was little more than a figurehead at this point, but nonetheless, he arrived in order to play his role, accompanied by young Caligula. The ceremony required him to throw a javelin. It had been decades since Tiberius had last lifted the small, sleek, wooden weapon; once upon a time, he had thrown them with deadly accuracy into the throats of Rome's enemies. His movements had been effortless then, young and lithe, his heart filled with passion for Vipsania and comradeship with Drusus. But now he was just an overweight, tired, drunken, old man, stumbling into the ceremony to throw this javelin and then hopefully get back to Capri for some more debauchery. Still, he'd prove to these people that he was still the emperor. Drawing his arm back, Tiberius flung the javelin as hard as he could. It was a terrible mistake. Agony popped through his right shoulder, and it was more than he could take. The emperor crumpled to the ground, and his attendants flocked around him in a panic.

For days, Tiberius failed to awaken from his coma. Kept comfortable in his villa at Misenum, he seemed to be slowly slipping away from the world that had treated him so harshly. By March 16th, even his breathing had stopped. Overjoyed, Caligula announced himself to be the new emperor; the people, in honor of their beloved Germanicus, were quick to hail him. They had no way of knowing that he would become a far worse emperor than his adopted grandfather had been; for now, they just hoped to have a more stable ruler than Tiberius had turned out to be. Waves of supporters began to make arrangements for Caligula to be crowned emperor.

It was to their horror that news arrived from Tiberius' villa. Not only was the old emperor not dead, but he was busy waking up—in fact, he was talking to his attendants. Panic spread through Misenum as Caligula's supporters realized that all of them had effectively committed treason. Droves of terrified people began to flee from the emperor's wrath, just as his family had once fled from the face of Augustus. As chaos filled the port city, Caligula remained calm. He ordered the commander of the Praetorian guard—his right-hand man, Macro—to deal with the problem. And in the midst of the panic, Macro marched calmly into Tiberius' bedroom, pushed aside his attendants, seized the old man's bedclothes, and suffocated him. Tiberius could do nothing to defend himself.

Tiberius was 77 years old when he died, and his rule had lasted for 23 years. Despite the fact that he had left Rome's coffers full to almost overflowing, and the empire much more stable than in the time of Augustus, his appalling behavior in the last eleven years of his reign had made him abundantly unpopular with the people and with history.

Conclusion

Tiberius was briskly succeeded by Caligula, who forced the former emperor's biological grandson, Tiberius Gemellus, out of his birthright to the throne. Caligula would become even more dreadful than Tiberius had been. After a promising start, Caligula became ill only a few months after beginning his rule. His body recovered, but his mind never did. Rome would suffer under the reign of a complete madman for the next four years until his own family stabbed him to death in 41 CE.

Tiberius himself would go down in history as Rome's second emperor, as well as one of the most unpopular Roman emperors. While he could not be described as a tyrant—more as a kind of deadbeat dad for an entire empire—the latter part of his reign was characterized by debauchery, lavish corruption, and absenteeism.

Yet reflecting on Tiberius' life before he became emperor, it is not difficult to see why he was driven to such lecherous lengths. His entire life had been controlled by Augustus; even in childhood, he was forced to accept that he had no say in how he grew up, who he married, or what his career path would be. He lost his beloved wife to Augustus' determination to secure the succession. He saw his brother killed in a war meant to expand Augustus' territory. And even when Augustus was gone, Tiberius found himself old and alone. He could think of nowhere else to turn than to all the ghastly pleasures he indulged in at Capri.

It bears mentioning that when Tiberius received the Roman Empire, it was still in its infancy. He was only the second emperor of Rome, ruling over a vast and sprawling territory that had recently been wracked by civil war, as Augustus used his sword's blade and sharp wit to beat a failing republic into a rising empire. Tiberius had the unenviable task of consolidating Rome, proving to the world that there was a Roman Empire even if Augustus was no longer alive. At that, at least, Tiberius was successful.

But despite the glittering early years of his reign, Tiberius had earned his reputation as one of Rome's worst emperors. Yet looking back on his sad life, and his horrible death, it has to be argued that he was also one of the most tragic.

Read more Captivating History Books about Ancient History

THE ROMAN EMPIRE

A CAPTIVATING GUIDE TO THE RISE AND FALL OF THE ROMAN EMPIRE INCLUDING STORIES OF ROMAN EMPERORS SUCH AS AUGUSTUS OCTAVIAN, TRAJAN, AND CLAUDIUS

CAPTIVATING HISTORY

Sources

https://www.rome.net/roman-republic

https://www.biography.com/political-figure/julius-caesar

https://www.ancient.eu/Lucius_Tarquinius_Superbus/

https://www.ancient.eu/Roman_Empire/

https://www.history.com/topics/ancient-rome/ancient-rome

https://www.thoughtco.com/the-early-kings-of-rome-119374

https://www.biography.com/political-figure/julius-caesar

https://www.ancient.eu/augustus/

https://www.nationalgeographic.com/culture/people/reference/augustus-caesar/

https://www.history.com/news/julius-caesar-assassin-ides-of-march

https://www.politico.com/story/2016/03/julius-caesar-is-assassinated-by-roman-senators-march-15-44-bc-220694

https://www.ancient.eu/Julius_Caesar/

https://www.history.com/topics/ancient-history/mark-antony

https://www.historyhit.com/the-last-civil-war-of-the-roman-republic/

https://www.ancient.eu/Livia_Drusilla/

https://www.britannica.com/biography/Nero-Claudius-Drusus-Germanicus

https://www.ancient.eu/article/96/the-roman-funeral/

https://www.nationalgeographic.com/culture/people/reference/augustus-caesar/

https://www.geni.com/people/Tiberius-Claudius-Nero/6000000003051269288

https://www.thefamouspeople.com/profiles/tiberius-4397.php

http://www.applet-magic.com/tiberius.htm

https://www.livius.org/search/?q=tiberius

https://www.livius.org/articles/person/julia-3/

https://www.historyofroyalwomen.com/roman-empire/julia-elder-biological-child-emperor-augustus/

https://www.geni.com/people/Nero-Claudius-Drusus-Germanicus/6000000007774655553

https://www.ancient.eu/Tiberius/

https://www.ancient.eu/Germanicus/

https://www.britannica.com/biography/Tiberius/Reign-as-emperor

https://www.ancient.eu/Livia_Drusilla/

https://www.ancientworldmagazine.com/articles/villa-jovis-tiberius-villa-capri/

https://blog.oup.com/2014/11/roman-emperor-tiberius-capri-suetonius/

http://blogs.nottingham.ac.uk/mintimperials/2015/03/16/on-this-day-in-37ad-the-roman-emperor-tiberius-died/

https://www.thoughtco.com/tiberius-roman-emperor-121262

https://www.history.com/topics/ancient-history/caligula

Illustration I: By Luis García (Zaqarbal), 25 March 2006., CC BY-SA 3.0, https://commons.wikimedia.org/w/index.php?curid=664161

Illustration II: This file comes from Wellcome Images, a website operated by Wellcome Trust, a global charitable foundation based in the United Kingdom. Refer to Wellcome blog post (archive).

Illustration III: https://upload.wikimedia.org/wikipedia/commons/6/6c/Tiberius_RPC_5089.jpg

www.ingramcontent.com/pod-product-compliance
Lightning Source LLC
LaVergne TN
LVHW042001060526
838200LV00041B/1821